Ocean Life
Tide Pool Creatures

Written by Alice Leonhardt

STECK-VAUGHN
C O M P A N Y

A Division of Harcourt Brace & Company

www.steck-vaughn.com

Contents

Chapter 1

What Is a Tide Pool?

A visit to the ocean is lots of fun. You can dig in the sand, lie in the sun, and splash in the waves. For many people the ocean is a place to visit. For many animals the ocean is home.

If you visit an ocean, look for a rocky shore. Take a walk among the rocks. Be careful, though. They may be wet and slippery. Look around. The area may appear empty, but is it? Bend down next to a deep pool of water that has collected in the rocks. This is called a tide pool.

A tide pool is made when the waves go out and some seawater stays behind, trapped in hollows and holes of the rocky shore. Look closely into the tide pool. If you're patient, you may see something silver dart from a **crevice,** or crack, in the rocks. A red "flower" may wave at you. A velvety rock might suddenly move.

Dozens of unusual animals make their home in tide pools. Some spend their whole life in a pool. Others spend part of their life in the ocean. But each tide pool **inhabitant** has learned to live in a home controlled by the ocean.

The ocean can make life in a tide pool difficult. All oceans have tides caused by the moon's pull on the water. During **high tide** the ocean waves rush to the shore. Tide pool animals must survive the pounding waves and rough sand. They must also survive hungry ocean **predators** eager to catch a tasty meal. During **low tide** the waves are pulled out toward the sea. The tide pool animals must survive the hot sun, drying winds, and hungry land predators.

The starfish and the anemone are brightly colored tide pool creatures.

The ocean also makes life possible in a tide pool. High tide brings food and oxygen to the inhabitants. The new water also helps keep the saltiness of the pool just right. Low tide washes away wastes. It also carries away animal eggs that need to hatch in the ocean.

Visiting a tide pool is like exploring a tiny ocean world. Find a comfortable spot on the rocks where you can sit. Then quietly watch and wait for a tide pool creature to show you how it survives in its special ocean home.

The sea anemone has a round body with a mouth in the middle.

Chapter 2
Flower Creatures

The first creature you might spot in a tide pool looks like a colorful flower. Its many "petals" wave in the water. It's so pretty that you may be tempted to touch it. Don't! It might sting you. It's not a flower at all. It's a sea anemone (uh NEM uh nee), an animal related to the jellyfish.

Sea anemones come in many colors. Most tide pool anemones like to live in the shadows. They slide their body into a crevice, where they hide.

Sea anemones are simple animals without eyes, ears, or a skeleton. They cannot move quickly to escape from predators or to catch food. But they have **adapted** to their tide pool home in many ways.

Like a jellyfish, the sea anemone has **tentacles** with tiny stinging cells. The tentacles surround the anemone's mouth, which is in the center of its body.

The sea anemone has a foot that acts like a suction cup. It uses the foot to attach itself to a rock. Then it waits for a small fish to swim past and brush a tentacle. One sting will stun the fish. The tentacles then pull the fish into the sea anemone's mouth. When the fish is in the sea anemone's mouth, it is killed with more stings.

When an anemone senses danger, it tucks its tentacles into its mouth. Then it looks like a blob of jelly or a round mushroom. When the tide goes out, the anemone also tucks its tentacles inside to trap precious water. Watch out, though. It can still sting!

Sea anemones with tentacles tucked inside

Chapter 3

Swimming Creatures

A tide pool can be a dangerous home for the many fish that live there. When a fish heads toward the surface, a seabird may fly down to snap it up. When it swims toward the bottom, an anemone waits with its stinging tentacles. The sun heats and dries up the water in their pool. The rushing surf pounds their small home. A heavy rain may change the amount of salt in the water. In order to survive, the many different tide pool fish must be fast, hardy, and able to adapt.

Shannies are tide pool fish that do not have scales. They are long, smooth, and slippery. They can slide easily into cracks and under rocks to find food and hide from enemies. Their spotted coloring helps them blend into the rocks and seaweed. If the low tide leaves them stranded, they can wriggle across bare rock to deeper water.

The shanny is one kind of tide pool fish.

The female shanny lays its eggs in a crevice. The male guards the eggs for about 8 weeks until they hatch.

The worm pipefish is as long and thin as a blade of grass. It can hide well in seaweed and other tide pool plants. An adult pipefish has bony plates under its skin. This armor protects it from predators. The female pipefish lays its eggs in a pouch on the male. The male pipefish carries the eggs in its pouch until they hatch.

Pipefish swim and rest straight up and down. They look like the plants they hide in.

A clingfish hanging on to a sea anemone

The clingfish has a sucker on its belly that allows it to hang on to rocks. When the ocean waves crash into the pool, the clingfish clings tightly. It won't get washed away. Like many tide pool fish, the clingfish has eyes high on its head. These eyes allow it to watch for predators that attack from above, such as seabirds.

A rockling hiding among tide pool rocks

Rocklings are another kind of tide pool fish. They leave the pool in the spring to lay their eggs in the ocean. The eggs develop into **larvae**. The larvae grow into young fish. At high tide a wave will wash them into a tide pool, where they will spend the rest of their life.

If you look closely at the bottom of a tide pool, you may spot a sea scorpion. This animal is one of the larger fish that live in tide pools. Its uneven coloring makes it hard to find. Its colors often shift from light to dark. In these two ways, the sea scorpion can **camouflage** itself. But when a small fish swims past, you'll be able to see the sea scorpion. Suddenly it will open its huge mouth to swallow its meal in one gulp.

The sea scorpion is one of the fiercest fish in a tide pool. It can scare away enemies with a whip of its sharp spines. It even has spines around its eyes.

Chapter 4
Are They Creatures?

While you're studying a tide pool, you might notice several shells stuck to the rocks. Perhaps you poke at them. They don't budge. You tap the hard covering. Is there something alive under the shells?

One of the shelled creatures is a limpet, a kind of ocean snail. The limpet has a hard shell that protects it from predators, sun, and drying winds. It is a champion rock-clinger. It has a strong foot that seals it to the rock. It can take as much as 70 pounds (32 kilograms) of pull to get a limpet off a rock. It clings so tightly that ocean waves cannot wash it away.

Limpets attach to tide pool rocks.

The limpet uses its rough tongue to graze on **algae** (al GEE). Algae are tiny water plants. The limpet makes a winding trail through the algae as it eats. Each limpet has a home base that it carves in the rocks. At night and at low tide, the limpet returns to its home, where it is safe.

A chiton (KY tuhn) is tough to spot because it blends in with the rocks it sticks to. A chiton is only $\frac{1}{2}$ inch to 1 inch long, and it looks like a turtle in its shell. The shell has overlapping plates so that it can bend. If

Most chitons have 8 overlapping plates.

a seabird picks up a chiton in its beak, the chiton curls into a hard ball.

The chiton also grazes on algae. Its teeth have a hard coating. The coating keeps the chiton's teeth from wearing down as it chews food.

The barnacle is another tide pool inhabitant with a shell. This funny creature spends its entire life standing on its head. It begins life as a larva that looks like a worm. The larva grows

Barnacles at low tide

into an adult. The barnacle sticks itself, head down, onto a rock. Next, it grows hard, razor-sharp plates around its body. It will stay glued to the same place for the rest of its life.

If you study a barnacle, you will see a tiny hole in the top of its shell, somewhat like a trap door. Feathery feelers stick out of the hole. These are the barnacle's feet. When the tide comes in, a barnacle uses its feet to kick tiny bits of food into its mouth. When the tide goes out, the barnacle closes its trap door. It makes sure there's enough water inside to breathe and stay moist.

Chapter 5

Creeping Creatures

The crab is another shelled animal that lives in a tide pool. Like a barnacle, the crab is protected by a hard outer shell. As the crab grows, it sheds its old skeleton. A new one is underneath.

Finding a crab in a tide pool is difficult. Crabs are shy and very fast. Like most tide pool creatures, they have coloring that helps camouflage them. To find a crab, look for something skittering sideways.

A velvet crab has red eyes.

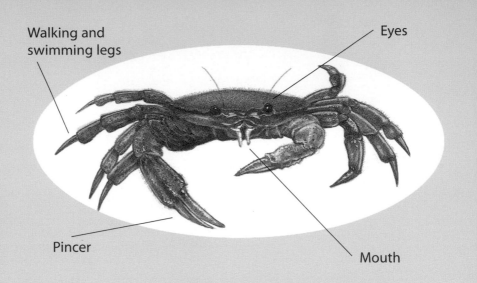

Walking and swimming legs

Eyes

Pincer

Mouth

A crab has five pairs of legs. Four pairs are for walking and swimming. When a crab walks, the walking and swimming legs on one side push. Those on the other side pull. This is why a crab walks sideways.

The fifth pair of legs have **pincers**. Many crabs are **scavengers**. They eat dead things. The pincers are used for picking up food. They are also used for attacking and defending. If the crab loses a pincer or a walking leg in a fight, it slowly grows another. If you see a crab rise up on its legs, watch out. It's ready to attack!

The velvet crab is a fierce hunter. Its bright red eyes and sharp blue pincers say "Beware!" The top part of the velvet crab's shell is covered with fine hairs. Very small bits of dirt become trapped in the hairs. The dirt helps to camouflage the crab when it is on the bottom of a tide pool.

The piecrust crab is another crab that lives in a tide pool. The top of its shell looks just like the crust of a pie. It is good to eat, and millions are caught every year. Only young piecrust crabs live in tide pools. The adult crabs leave with the tide to live in deeper ocean water.

The piecrust crab has very fine hairs on its legs. These hairs help the crab feel its way along the cracks and crevices of the tide pool.

The piecrust crab is also called the edible crab because it is good to eat.

One odd creature you can find in a tide pool is the hermit crab. A hermit is someone who lives alone, away from other people. The name *hermit* is also given to many animals that live alone. The hermit crab is one of these animals.

The hermit crab has a hard shell only in front. To protect the rear part of its body, it must "borrow" a shell. First it finds an empty shell. Then it backs into it.

The crab's two pairs of hind legs are made especially for hanging onto the inside of a shell. Its two pairs of front legs are used for walking. As it travels, the crab drags its home behind it. As it grows, it looks for a bigger shell to move into.

The hermit crab also has a pair of pincers. The right one is usually bigger than the left. If the hermit crab is attacked by a hungry seabird, it backs into its shell. It holds the right pincer in front like a door. This keeps the seabird's sharp beak from getting inside. Sometimes low tide leaves the hermit crab stranded. Then the crab closes itself into its borrowed shell to keep from drying out.

This hermit crab has borrowed a dog whelk shell.

A lobster stranded in a tide pool

Many tide pool creatures are just visitors. If you get a chance to study different pools, you may not see them. They may have been swept back to their ocean home by the waves.

One such visitor is the lobster. It usually lives in the ocean. Sometimes a small one will become stranded in a tide pool. It will hide during the day and then come out at night. It eats other animals, crushing the meat with its claws. If a predator attacks, the lobster rapidly fans its tail to make a fast backwards escape.

Chapter 6

Spiny Creatures

One of the most unusual creatures in a tide pool is the sea star, or starfish. A starfish is not really a fish. It does not have gills or fins. Parts of its skeleton stick out of its skin in spines on the tops of its arms. The spines help protect it from predators. Some starfish have tiny pincers around their spines. The pincers clean the arms, picking off unwanted dirt and seaweed.

A starfish getting ready to eat a clam

On the underside of its arms, a starfish has hundreds of feet. Each foot is a round tube filled with fluid. The feet push and pull together to help the starfish move. If a wave flips the starfish over, its tiny feet will grip a rock. The starfish will slowly turn itself back over.

The tip of each starfish arm has an eyespot that can sense light and dark. Small tentacles on each tip can sense sounds and smells. If an arm breaks off, the starfish can grow a new one. In fact, from just one arm and a small piece of the body, a starfish can regrow itself!

When a starfish enters a tide pool, all the other creatures hide. A starfish has a huge appetite. It eats the limpets and barnacles in tide pools. It also eats clams that it finds on the beach. Using its strong arms, a starfish can pry open even a tough clamshell. It pushes its stomach into the shell. The stomach digests the clam. Then the starfish pulls its stomach back into its body. What an interesting way to eat dinner!

Starfish can have anywhere from 3 to 50 arms. Most have 5.

The sea urchin is related to the starfish. Both have spiny skin. The sea urchin's spines protect it from predators. Some of the spines have poisonous pincers on the ends. The pincers can break off and stick to an attacker. They inject poison into the attacker's skin. The sea urchin can regrow any spines that break.

Like the starfish, the sea urchin also has hundreds of feet. They lie in rows between the spines. The feet help the urchin climb rocks and cling tightly when ocean waves crash over it.

Even though sea urchins are colorful, they are often hard to find. Look in the cracks and crevices of the tide pool rocks. Sometimes the urchin uses its spines to scrape a hole to hide in. Sometimes it uses its feet to hold seaweed, pebbles, and small shells on its body. In this way it can blend into its surroundings and hide from predators.

A sea urchin eats plants and animals. Its mouth is on the bottom of its body. Using its feet, it pulls itself along the rocks in the tide pool.

The mouth scrapes food from the rocks. Too many sea urchins can scrape the rocks clean, leaving them bare.

Sea urchins look like round balls covered with spines.

If you hunt along the rocky shore, you might find a dead sea urchin. All that will be left is the hard, round skeleton. The inside will be empty because the sea urchin's soft inner body parts will have been eaten or will have rotted. This fragile skeleton is sometimes called the jewel box of the sea because of its beauty. It is very fragile, so handle it with care.

Chapter 7
Sluggish Creatures

While you're studying a tide pool, you might spot a long yellow-brown blob clinging to some seaweed. Perhaps you spy another blob with a bushy back. Neither looks like a plant, nor does it look like an animal. These strange creatures are sea slugs. They are members of the mollusk family, which includes clams, mussels, oysters, snails, and octopuses. Some mollusks, like snails, have shells. Others, like sea slugs, do not have shells.

Sea slugs don't move fast, and they have no shell for protection. How do they survive in a world full of predators? Most blend in with the seaweed. Some have stinging cells they get from the anemones that they eat. Many taste horrible and have bright colors. Their bright colors warn predators to stay away.

The sea slug is a snail without a shell.

During high tide the sea slugs get oxygen from the seawater. Some breathe through their skin. Others use gills located on their back. High tide is also when the sea slug comes out to eat. Creeping along, it sometimes uses its coarse tongue to scrape food off the seaweed or rocks.

During low tide the sea slug must find shelter from the dry air and hot sun. The slug has to keep its body moist just like a snail does. It hunts for a damp crevice or clump of seaweed and waits for high tide to come once again.

Sea slugs lay thousands of eggs in the ocean. Many will be eaten before they hatch. The sea lemon lays its eggs in a long, flat coil that may have as many as 500,000 eggs! The eggs hatch into larvae. The larvae swim in the ocean until they grow into adults. Then they head toward the shore, where some will be washed into tide pools by the waves.

Chapter 8

Two-Shelled Creatures

One creature you can often see in a tide pool is a mussel. Because its shell has 2 halves that can open and close, it is called a **bivalve.**

Mussels live in groups called colonies. From eggs they hatch into tiny larvae. The larvae search for a spot on a warm, wet rock. They attach

A colony of mussels in a tide pool.

themselves to the rock with strong threads on their foot. Then they build their shell.

While the mussels are growing, the many threads on their foot keep them stuck to the rock, even when powerful waves wash over them. Later in their life, the mussels use their foot to move slowly from spot to spot to find food or protection.

If you study a colony of mussels at low tide, you'll think they are not alive. The mussels don't move. The two halves of their shell are tightly closed. But when the tide comes in, the mussels open their shell to let the ocean water in.

To eat, a mussel draws seawater into its shell. Using tiny hairs called cilia (SIL ee uh), it filters out bits of food in the seawater. The food goes into the mussel's digestive system, while the seawater is passed out.

Chapter 9
Hunter Creatures

Among a colony of mussels, you might spy a slow creature with a colorful shell. This is a dog whelk.

Also called sea snails, whelks build spiral shells. The shells can be yellow, pink, orange, or purple. If its shell is dark, a whelk has been eating mussels. If the shell is pale, it has been eating barnacles. A mixed diet creates a striped shell.

The whelk builds a shell to protect its soft body. As it grows, it adds more shell to the open end. The whelk can seal itself inside the shell. If the whelk gets washed onto the shore, it closes its "door" to help keep itself safe from predators.

The dog whelk is a slow but busy hunter. It creeps along the rocks, searching for mussels, barnacles, and limpets. Because it hunts animals that don't move, the whelk doesn't need to be a quick, ferocious hunter.

These dog whelks have laid the egg capsules at their right.

When a whelk eats a mussel, it pushes its **proboscis** inside the shell. The proboscis is a hollow tube for feeding. Then the whelk uses its rough tongue to scrape out the soft flesh of the mussel. The tongue can also drill holes through a shell that has been softened by a special chemical the whelk makes. Even when the shell is softened, drilling the hole may take as long as 3 days.

The female dog whelk lays about 10 egg capsules in the cracks or under the rocks of the tide pool. Each capsule contains about 1000 eggs. Only 20 to 30 of the eggs hatch. The other eggs are used for food by the ones that will hatch.

Tiny whelks hatch out after about 4 months. They hide in a safe place. When they are bigger, they begin to hunt for other creatures to eat.

Another hunter in tide pools is the baby octopus. It is often washed into a pool at high tide. Don't scare it! An octopus is very shy. It will squirt out water to make a speedy escape. It may also squirt out dark ink to hide itself.

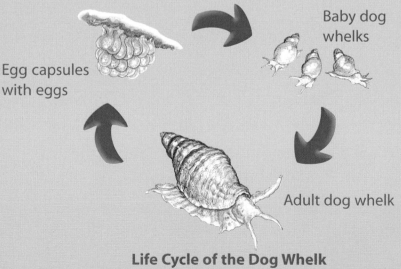

Egg capsules with eggs

Baby dog whelks

Adult dog whelk

Life Cycle of the Dog Whelk

The octopus has a well-developed brain. It also has excellent eyesight. It can see at night, which is when it hunts. Sometimes it attracts a crab by wiggling the tip of one arm. When the crab comes near, the octopus pounces. Then it sticks its beak into the crab. It kills the crab by injecting poison into its shell.

Each arm of an octopus has two rows of suckers.

Chapter 10

Life in a Tide Pool

Life in a tide pool is tricky. The inhabitants are pounded by waves. They are stranded by low tides, dunked by high tides, and hunted by predators on land and in the ocean. But the tide pool is still a home for many creatures.

As you watch the creatures in a tide pool, you will be able to understand the food chain of the pool. The limpet eats the algae. The starfish eats the limpet. The shanny eats the starfish eggs. The sea scorpion eats the shanny. And the crab cleans up the leftovers.

Seabirds eat many kinds of tide pool creatures.

Sometimes tide pool creatures depend on each other. If you see a hermit crab, you may notice a passenger on its shell. The passenger is a small sea anemone. The hermit crab and the anemone often live as partners. The sea anemone clings to the hermit crab's shell. When the hermit crab travels, it carries the sea anemone to new feeding places. The sea anemone catches bits of food left by the hermit crab. In return, the sea anemone helps hide the crab's shell. It also protects the crab with its stinging tentacles.

Animals that live in tide pools often look strange, compared to animals that live on land. Many tide pool creatures don't have eyes, ears, hair, skin, or bones. Why? They have had to adapt to living both in and out of the ocean. Limpets developed a trap door that they use to catch and hold seawater. Barnacles glue themselves onto rocks so that they won't be washed out to sea. The shanny is narrow and slippery so that it can wriggle across bare rock to find water.

To survive, the animals have also had to develop ways to deal with the changing tides. Twice a day, day after day, the tide turns. Each animal must sense the shifting tide before it's too late. Some cling to the rocks with special feet. Some slip into damp crevices. All need a way to survive the changing conditions.

If you ever visit a tide pool, enjoy your visit. You will discover that beneath the calm surface of the water is a tiny ocean world brimming with life.

Glossary

adapt to adjust

algae water plants that make their own food

bivalve a mollusk with a hinged shell, such as a clam

camouflage to hide

crevice a narrow crack or opening

high tide the time of day when the moon pulls the ocean toward the shore

inhabitant an animal that lives in a place

larvae the newly hatched young of some animals

low tide the time of day when the moon pulls the ocean away from the shore

pincer a jointed claw

predator an animal that kills another for food

proboscis a tube that some animals use for feeding

scavenger an animal that feeds on the remains of plants or animals

tentacle a narrow, armlike part of some animals